Tame Your Tongue & Transform Your Relationship

Dr. Linda G. Wiley

Copyright © 2012 Dr. Linda G. Wiley
All rights reserved.

ISBN: 1-4610-6007-9
ISBN-13: 9781461060079

Dedication

This book is dedicated to all of the men and women
upon whose shoulders I stand.
To those who are standing beside me,
And to those who will, one day, find me worthy to be a
part of their foundation.
Stand tall.

Acknowledgements

I give thanks to God, the Creator of all things and to His Son, Jesus Christ, who is in control of my life.
I thank my mother who gave me life and taught me that, through Christ, I can do all things.
I thank my children who literally kept me alive during the dark times of my life. I thank my husband who inspired me in ways that he may never know.
Thanks to my family and friends for their support and to the people who were not always on my side, for it is through adversity that we learn to appreciate life.

Many people have helped me to become the person that I am today. Some of them played an active role in the development of this book. Whether you helped me develop the concept, made suggestions, edited, encouraged, listened to me whine, or spoke life into me and the book, I am grateful. Many of you helped and don't even know it, but God knows and He is pleased.
Thank you!

Be blessed!

Table of Contents

Acknowledgements	v
Foreword	ix
Introduction	xi
Chapter 1: We were meant to be in relationships	1
Chapter 2: Which tounge is yours?	15
Chapter 3: The Conniving Tongue	39
Chapter 4 : The Careless Tongue	53
Chapter 5 : The Controlled Tongue	67
Chapter 6: : The Caring Tongue	79
Chapter 7 : Why Tame Your Tongue?	89
Chapter 8 : How to Tame Your Tongue	97
Afterthought	107
Appendix 1: About the author	111

Appendix 2: Workshops   113

Appendix 3: How to order books and
    other products   115

"And be not conformed to this world; but be ye transformed by the renewing of your mind, that ye may prove what is the good, and acceptable, and perfect, will of God."
Romans 12:2 (KJV)

Introduction

As far back as Aunt Esther of *Sanford and Son* fame, we have applauded the attitude slinging, insult flinging black woman. We have credited characters like Willona Woods (*Good Times*), Florence the maid (*The Jeffersons*), Nikki Parker (*The Parkers*), Toni Childs (*Girlfriends*), and Ma'Dea (*Diary of a Mad Black Woman*) with being independent, savvy, confident, and in charge. We've repeated their sayings; emulated their styles. Our children have been exposed to them as if they are, or should be, studied as role models. We've even extended our admiration to a few white women, such as, Rhoda Morgenstern (*The Mary Tyler Moore Show*) and Roseanne's sister Jackie (*Roseanne*) . These women have been the topic of discussion during plenty of "girls' night" outings. They are funny and not to be ignored. These women are funny, but they are not in healthy relationships. Yes, they may get the laughter, but do they get the man?

This book was written primarily for women. Therefore, many of the examples will be written from a woman's perspective. Why? First of all, it is a book on communication styles and women typically do more talking than men. We all know from countless books, movies, and personal experiences that women are from Venus, a planet that is apparently far more talkative then Mars, Earth, or any other planet in our solar system. Consequently, if I inform a woman she will inform her man. She can't help it! She will want him to know of this new information that she has found. Women like for men to know how smart they are. She will want him to know how she plans to apply it to her life, to his life, and to their relationship. And, of course, she will want him to know how she plans for him to apply it also! Women have a propensity for wanting to change people. Therefore, if I educate the woman in a couple, I have in effect, informed both parties.

Secondly, women have a reputation — deserved or undeserved — for tearing people down with their tongues. When their hands begin to flail and their necks begin to roll you better get out of the way! Women, more often than men, have been called mouthy, catty, backbiting and a host of other unflattering adjectives. Women would rather tell than be told. As a defense mechanism, women tend to attack rather than allow themselves to be attacked or even feel vulnerable to attack. Since far too many women experience a less than optimal level of self esteem, they feel subject to attack much of the time. Therefore, they strike first and hard.

Finally, this book was written primarily for women because I am interested in, and committed to, the process of improving the psychological condition of women. Women are, more often than men, overlooked

Tame Your Tongue and Transform Your Relationship

and under rated in the workplace, in the home, and in society in general. This affects their self esteem and is often demonstrated in their behavior. It makes some women lie down and play dead. You know the type; the woman who never has an original thought or idea of her own. She seems to exist only to agree with everything her man says. She would lose herself if she thought it would make him love her more.

Well, excuse me, but she is not the focus of this discussion. I do not want to address the type of women who lie down and play dead, but the type who stand up and roar! Being overlooked and under rated makes some women appear hard and independent. This type of woman appears to have it all together. She never asks for help; come to think of it, she never feels she needs help. She never cries, rarely laughs, and thinks that most people's idea of fun and relaxation is nothing more than a big waste of time.

The impact of being overlooked and under rated makes some women appear dominant and unwilling to submit. She is the type of woman who has to have the first word, the last word and almost every word in between. She doesn't approve of any idea except her own. This type of woman won't let anyone tell her what to do and she rarely sees value in the opinions of others.

Some women respond to being overlooked and under rated by becoming apparently more confident, even to the extreme of being conceited. This type of woman is very demanding and wants her way at all times. She expects a man to cater to her and refuses to compromise. In a healthy relationship, compromise is key. It does not mean losing your personality to the personality of another, but it does mean that there is compatibility and mutual respect.

I am committed to improving the self esteem of women and positively influencing the family dynamic. One way to do this is by changing the way men and women communicate. Positive talk produces positive results.

But if you are a man, do not despair and *do not* close this book! It is written for you, too. You see gentlemen, whether you like it or not, you are the people that women frequently talk *at* and talk *to*. Wouldn't it be helpful to understand their communication styles a little better? Wouldn't it be helpful to understand the thinking that influences *their* thinking? It's like the secret decoder ring you had as a child. *Tame Your Tongue & Transform Your Relationship* will help you break the communication code. You will learn why you feel the way you do when she speaks. You will understand why she speaks the way she does and, perhaps more importantly, how to help her change her tongue. I cannot help women without helping the people in their world and that, gentlemen, includes you.

Tame Your Tongue and Transform Your Relationship

Secondly, gentlemen, this book is for you because it will allow you to anticipate the changes that she will make to her communication style and the changes she may desire in you. You will have the opportunity to apply the wisdom from these pages and change the way you communicate before she tries to do it!

Communication is a two way street. Men, you also have communication styles. *Tame Your Tongue & Transform Your Relationship* will increase your understanding of yourself. You will be able to determine your communication style and how to communicate more effectively with your woman and other people around you. Women love men who are supportive and encouraging of their words. What you learn by reading *Tame Your Tongue & Transform Your Relationship* will definitely help you.

We each have a communication style that impacts how effectively we interact with others. You may talk more than others. Perhaps you are more of a listener. Maybe you think only of yourself at times when you should act with compassion. What we *say* probably affects more people than any other action we take. It is not surprising, then, to find that the Bible book of Proverbs gives special attention to words and how they are used. *Tame Your Tongue & Transform Your* Relationship identifies four communication styles, communication styles that I refer to as tongues. These are tongues of well-intentioned, yet sometimes misguided saints like you and I; righteous people striving to get it right. Each of us has a tendency to communicate based on one of these four tongues. The way you typically speak is a true measure of who you are because the tongue reveals the heart.

"For out of the overflow of the heart the mouth speaks. The good man brings good things out of the good stored up in him, and the evil man brings evil things out of the evil stored up in him." (Matthew 12:34-35) [NIV]

What is stored up inside of you? We all fall short of God's glory and need to improve upon the ways in which we speak to one another. *Tame Your Tongue & Transform Your Relationship* is designed to help. It is written with three objectives in mind.

- To help you determine your primary tongue
- To help you understand how your tongue impacts your interactions with others
- To introduce ways to develop a more positive communication style

Tame Your Tongue and Transform Your Relationship

Read on. You will gain a new perspective, transform the way you think and the way you speak, and find a significant improvement in the quality of your relationships. Read on and learn how to tame your tongue and transform your relationships

> *"Death and life are in the power of the tongue; and they that love it shall eat the fruit thereof."*
> *Proverbs 18:21 (KJV)*

Chapter 1
We were meant to be in relationships

"The Lord God said, "It is not good for the man to be alone. I will make a helper suitable for him." (Genesis 2:18) [NIV]

From the beginning, God intended for man to be in relationships. This is demonstrated early in the book of Genesis.

"So God created man in his own image, in the image of God he created him; male and female he created them. God blessed them and said to them, "Be fruitful and increase in number: fill the earth and subdue it." (Genesis 1:27-28 (a)) [NIV]

God made man to have fruitful relationships. A fruitful relationship is one that is abundant, plentiful, and produces much. A relationship cannot be accomplished without communication and a healthy relationship requires healthy communication. Communication is the most talked about and least understood area of human behavior. It is the transfer of information in the form of ideas, wants, desires, feelings, and much more. Effective communication is crucial in relationships of all types — friendship, professional, family, romantic — yet, it is rarely taught and even more rarely learned in our society.

Interpersonal communication includes the following elements:
1. A sender. Someone who wants to "send" a message verbally or non-verbally to someone else.
2. A receiver. Someone who will "receive" a message from another person.
3. A message. Information in some form.
4. Noise. Anything that interferes or causes the deletion, distortion or generalization of the exact replication of information being transmitted from the mind of the sender to the mind of the receiver.
5. Feedback. Both the sender and receiver constantly elicit verbal and nonverbal feedback to the other person.
6. Replication. The duplication of understanding in one person that is in the mind of another person. Replication is an approximate goal and philosophically not perfectly possible, though desired.
7. Understanding. An approximation of what the message means to the sender by the receiver.

8. Impact. The effect of the message on the receiver.

Ineffective communication can create a block in the relationship. The degree of the block can vary depending on how severe or how often the ineffective communication is delivered. No matter what we actually say to other people, our words and the manner in which we express them, also send messages about what we think of them, what we think of ourselves, and whether or not we are being sincere and genuine in what we say.

Shannon is a 35 year old female in relationship with John, a 37 year old male. She and John have been arguing because John broke a date with her in order to hang out with his best friend and his best friend's cousin. Shannon needs to convey her disapproval to John.

Example:

Sender	Shannon
Receiver	John
Message	You were wrong to break our date
Noise	Hurt, anger, jealousy, frustration
Feedback	Comments, questions, clarifications, facial expressions, body language during the exchange
Replication	(Would only occur if John believes what Shannon believes -- that he was wrong to break the date.)
Understanding	Knowing that Shannon believes he was wrong to break the date. Understanding does not mean agreement.
Impact	The effect of the message on the receiver

Tame Your Tongue and Transform Your Relationship

Each communication exchange follows the same format as detailed above. However, not every communication exchange has the same style. By "style" I am referring to the pattern of words, motives, and intended outcomes. Each style has it's own resulting effect on the receiver of the message.

We each have a communication style that we tend to use most often. It is the style that flows naturally. We use it without even thinking. For example, scripture makes reference to four communication styles that I refer to as tongues. These are the tongues of well-intentioned people. Two of the four tongues cause pain and destruction to the fabric of our relationships while the other two do just the opposite. They help to build and uplift. Two of the styles should be emulated while the other two should be avoided.

What causes some of us to speak in ways that hurt and destroy? The answer is fear: fear of being hurt, physically and/or emotionally, fear of disappointment, fear of rejection, fear of abandonment, fear of not being good enough, fear of being too good, fear of failure, fear of caring, fear of success, fear of the unknown, and fear of intimacy. As we experience things in life, residual effects stay with us. We refer to these effects as "baggage" – stuff that we pack away in our hearts, minds, and souls. Some baggage is positive. It is in the form of happy memories and pleasant times. Some baggage is negative. It reminds us of pains that we would rather forget. Accumulating baggage is a natural phenomenon; however, all baggage – positive and negative – has the potential to get in the way of effective communication and can close your mind to new experiences. Baggage leads to fear. Fear results in the use of negative tongues.

People act out of fear if they have:
- been chronically put down for the way they feel or for what they believe.
- been emotionally hurt in the past and are not willing to risk getting hurt in the future.
- had problem relationships in the past where they were belittled, misunderstood, or ignored.
- experienced the death of a loved one resulting in unresolved grief and the inability to open up to others, due to the fear of being left alone again due to death or abandonment.
- experienced a hostile or bitter divorce, separation, or end of a relationship.
- lived in an environment emotionally or physically unpredictable and volatile.
- low self-esteem and cannot believe that they are deserving of the attention, care, and concern of anyone.

These types of experiences cause us to operate in a reactionary mode most of the time. We react as if we are still in the painful situation that caused us to fear in the first place. For example, if you have experienced relation-

Tame Your Tongue and Transform Your Relationship

ships in which someone repeatedly ignored or belittled you, you struggled to find ways to be noticed. Perhaps you began to dress in flamboyant or provocative ways. Maybe you took on a comedic personality and began telling jokes at someone else's expense. Or maybe you assumed the behavior of lashing out with your tongue. If experience taught you that someone, perhaps everyone, is out to get you, you may have developed a mindset of "getting them before they get you." Perhaps experience taught you that men cannot be trusted so you must say or do whatever it takes to get what you need and want. More often than not, we "get people and our way" with the words that we use and the manner in which we use them. We "get" these things with our tongues.

During the course of any given day, you are faced with experiences that challenge your patience; experiences that take you back to past situations and possibly past hurts. Here are some examples: your children make you late for work and now you will have to face the authority figures on your job. Without realizing it, having to face the boss might remind you of times when you had to face other authority figures in life who belittled you. Or a driver on the interstate cuts you off. That action might subconsciously trigger thoughts of being overlooked and ignored and the pain that went with it. Or your boss denies your vacation request but approves vacation for your co-worker. If there were times in your life when a man cheated or favored another woman over you, this might trigger that pain. And the list of challenges goes on and on and on.

When the children make you late, will you demonstrate patience and show them compassion or will you strike out from your fear of returning to an emotionally volatile environment? Will you speak harshly to the children and make them feel bad? At that moment, you have an opportunity to demonstrate patience and ease their anxiety or cast darkness on their day causing the cycle to continue. Perhaps the driver who cut you off on the interstate was distracted by the pressures of his day. Maybe she didn't see you until after she started moving into your lane. She may not have intended to cut you off. You can exercise control and ignore the action or you can say something to her to assert your presence and further ruin her day. As for your boss, give him the benefit of the doubt. There may be a good reason for his decision. Managing people with different needs is a complex responsibility. There is a lot to consider like coverage of responsibilities, who asked first, proper attitude, length of time on the job, etc. Use your words to find out rather than to talk about him to your friends.

Practice separating events from your emotions. In other words, a "no" is just a "no." Do not take it personally. You don't know what it means unless you ask. Avoid making up your own interpretation about the actions of others. The interpretation may cause you to act out of character. If negative, it certainly will interfere with your ability to communicate from a spirit of love. Your response affects the way people perceive you and, therefore, the way they will treat you in the moment

Tame Your Tongue and Transform Your Relationship

and in the future. Your words are directly related to the quality of your relationships.

If you often feel as if co-workers, family members, or your mate are speaking in a negative manner towards you or putting you down, maybe you should look at the one person common to all of those relationships – you. This is not a put down. It is an invitation to look in the mirror and enhance the beautiful reflection that is you. If you are critical rather than compassionate, you will also receive criticism. If you treat others generously, graciously, and compassionately, however, these qualities will come back to you in full measure.

Why do we speak to people anyway? From friendly advice to impassioned speeches, messages are sent and received with each sender trying to impart information, knowledge, or wisdom. In other words, we speak to communicate ideas and feelings. We speak to achieve certain desired results. If you use an ineffective manner, chances are you will not communicate accurately and will, therefore, not get the results that you desire. The listener will not receive the intended message. In fact, you may create an uncomfortable or hostile environment.

Where do these communication styles come from? Speech is an action. Actions are based on thoughts. Thoughts are derived from the information we allow to enter our minds. What you put into your mind determines what comes out in your words.

Dr. Linda G. Wiley

In his letter to the church at Philippi, the Apostle Paul tells us all to program our minds with thoughts that are true, noble, right, pure, lovely, admirable, excellent, and praiseworthy.

"Finally, brothers, whatever is true, whatever is noble, whatever is right, whatever is pure, whatever is lovely, whatever is admirable – if anything is excellent or praiseworthy – think about such things." (Philippians 4:8) [NIV]

If your thoughts are true, noble, right, pure, lovely, admirable, excellent, and praiseworthy, your words to others will be also.

How often do you find yourself operating on assumption or speculation rather than truth? Probably more often than you realize. Let's say for example, your husband comes home late from work without calling. What thoughts does that generate in your mind? When he arrives at home do you accuse him of being out with friends having a good time? Do you call him inconsiderate? Isn't this all based on assumption and speculation? You really don't *know* at that point where he was, what he was doing, or why he was unable to call. These unfounded thoughts may lead you to call him hurtful names, attack his character, and so on. Instead of attacking him on the night that he comes home late without calling, try thanking him on all of the other nights when he comes home at a reasonable time or when he remembers to call to inform you that he will be late.

Tame Your Tongue and Transform Your Relationship

Ask, out of concern rather than accusation, if he is okay and let it go at that.

What if you call your wife's cell phone repeatedly and she does not answer? Do you assume that she is avoiding your calls? Perhaps you think she is somewhere she shouldn't be with someone she shouldn't be with. These unfounded assumptions in your mind determine what comes out of your mouth. This may lead you to try to manipulate her to behave the way you want her to behave, you know: "I want you to keep your phone on at all times in case I need to reach you." "I need you to call and tell me what's going on throughout your day." Sometimes he sweetens it with, "I love hearing from you boo. Call me when you leave the hair salon" (and the office, and the mall, and your girlfriend's house.)

Where do all of these thoughts come from? When you watch a movie in which one spouse is cheating on another, that thought of unfaithful spouses is now in your mind. As soon as your spouse does something that the character in the movie did (come home late or turn off a cell phone), you begin to think they will do everything that the movie character did even though you haven't thought about that movie in weeks!

Perhaps a friend tells you why "so-and-so" at the church is getting a divorce and warns you to watch out for similar things in your own marriage. That plants seeds or thoughts in your mind. Examine what you allow to enter your mind through television, books, movies, music, and conversations. Replace harmful input with wholesome input. Read God's Word daily and pray. Guard your mind. Ask God to help you focus your thoughts on what is good and pure. It takes practice, but it can be done. Remember, "For as he thinketh in his heart, so is he." (Proverbs 23:7a) [KJV] The Good News Bible puts it this way, "What he thinks is what he really is." What you say and what you don't say are both important. Communicating effectively means not only saying the right words at the right time, but also controlling your desire to say things you should not say.

Our contradictory speech often puzzles us. At times our words are right and pleasing to God. At other times they are violent and destructive. Which of these communication tendencies reflects our true identity? The tongue gives us a picture of our basic human nature. We were made in God's image, but we have also fallen into sin. God works to change us from the inside out. When the Holy Spirit purifies a heart, he gives self-control so that the person will speak words that please God.

A relationship is a connection and exchange between people. Communication plays a large role in that exchange. We transmit information in the form of ideas, wants, desires, feelings, and much more. Incomplete communication can create a block in the relationship. The size and strength of the block vary depending

Tame Your Tongue and Transform Your Relationship

on how destructive the communication, or lack of communication, happens to be.

As we go through life, we have plenty of opportunities to be discouraged-times of indecision, loneliness, loss of employment or revenue, loss of loved ones. How we act in such situations will reflect who we are.

In the Bible, the book of 1 Samuel tells the story of Hannah, the beloved wife of Elkinah. No one was more discouraged then Hannah. To her dismay, Hannah could not bear children. Elkanah also had a second wife named Peninnah. Peninnah, jealous because Hannah was the favorite wife, often teased Hannah because "the Lord had shut up her womb" (1 Samuel 1:6). A much anticipated occasion was when Hannah, Elkanah, and other members of the family returned to the hills at Shiloh. Though she was her husband's favorite wife, those journeys to Shiloh were trying ones for Hannah. As she saw parents and children coming together, she grieved more deeply because she had no part in the parenting experience.

As her husband made his sacrifice in the tabernacle, he would give portions to his other wife, Peninnah, and to her sons and daughters. Though he gave Hannah an extra portion it was still much smaller because she had no children. Each year it became a hard experience emotionally for Hannah to make the journey to Shiloh. Finally on one trip she cried and would not eat. Elkanah, a sensitive man, asked her why she cried and why she would not eat. "Am I not more to you than ten sons?" (1 Samuel 1:8)

There was no answer from Hannah, but we know that she went into the tabernacle to pour out the anguish of her soul. And the prayer that she prayed has become one of the great petitions of a mother. Despite her situation and the continual torment from Peninnah, Hannah did not let this bad situation lead to bad behavior on her part. Though grieved in spirit, she kept her suffering to herself.

Hannah had a gift inside of her. Her gift was Samuel who would become Israel's greatest judge. She could not release her gift because of the bitterness inside of her.

God has given us all gifts and talents to be used for His glory. Oftentimes we cannot walk in our gifts because something inside of us gets in the way. What is your gift? Is it the next great breakthrough in technology or medicine? Is it a great song or a good book? Perhaps your gift is the next great leader of our people. Maybe it's a healthy and happy marriage. Have you given birth to God's best gift to you? If not, what is getting in your way?

Chapter 2
Which tongue is yours?

We all have the capacity to speak in each of the four tongues and we do, depending on our mood, where we are, and who we are speaking to. In my profession I focus on building better relationships, therefore, I speak with a caring tongue. However, in an argument with a friend, my tongue often becomes careless. It's not planned, it just happens.

Think how much more effective you could be if you knew:
- Which tongue you typically use
- How your tongue impacts others
- How to navigate from the use of one tongue to another

To begin, you must identify your primary tongue. We can all adapt our tongues if necessary, and we do, but there is one that we use most often. We may use a different tongue at work than we do at home. Or we might use a different tongue when we are happy versus when we are angry. Often we choose a different

Dr. Linda G. Wiley

tongue for those we love versus those we dislike. However, if we ask those who know us best, they could probably find some commonality in our tongues across all of those situations.

Following is an assessment that measures how much your natural communication resembles a particular tongue. Read each statement and decide how much it describes you. If it does not describe you at all, write "1" for "strongly disagree" in the space provided. If it describes you a little, write "2" for "disagree." If you can't decide because you only act that way about 50% of the time, write "3" for "neutral." If you agree with the statement because it describes how you are more often than not, write "4." If it describes you very well, write "5" for "strongly agree".

When you have responded to all of the statements, add up your scores for each of the four categories, A through D. Record each category score in the space provided. The highest score will indicate the tongue you most often use when you speak.

Tame Your Tongue and Transform Your Relationship

Instructions. Read each statement. On the line following the statement, place a number 1, 2, 3, 4 or 5 to indicate your level of agreement with the statement. Be sure to rate all 40 statements.

Strongly Disagree	Disagree	Neutral	Agree	Strongly Agree
1	2	3	4	5

A. I usually know the right words to say to comfort or encourage others _____

B. I have to have the last word. _____

C. I say whatever I need to in order to reach my goal. _____

D. I think about the impact of my words before I speak. _____

A. I am a compassionate person. _____

B. I am eager to give my opinion in any conversation. _____

C. I prefer to protect another's feelings rather than tell the absolute truth. _____

D. Most people find me trustworthy. _____

A. I speak up to make people feel better. _____

B. I repeat information even if I haven't verified that it is true. _____

C. I don't let people know exactly what I'm thinking. _____
D. Rather than retaliate, I respond in a positive way after being insulted. _____

A. I always try to speak the truth. _____
B. I often regret what I say after I say it. _____
C. It's not always possible to tell the truth. _____
D. I avoid talking too much about myself. _____

A. I strive to encourage others. _____

B. I say what I feel regardless of how it makes others feel. _____
C. I often share stories of my achievements. _____
D. I do not respond to anger with anger. _____

A. I find joy in speaking well of others. _____
B. I prefer to deal with a situation when it happens rather than walk away and address it later when things calm down. _____
C. I often tell my friends hearsay that I learn about others. _____
D. I am often sought out for my advice. _____

Tame Your Tongue and Transform Your Relationship

A. I show friendship by giving advice. _____
B. When someone annoys me I tell them about it. _____
C. If I don't like you, you will never know it by my behavior. _____
D. I am a pretty even-tempered person. _____

A. I do not use words that tear people down. _____
B. I don't let my negative feelings about others show. _____
C. My intentions are frequently misunderstood. _____
D. I try not to speak unless I am informing, encouraging, or teaching in a positive way. _____

A. I do not listen to or spread gossip. _____
B. I sometimes hurt people with my words. _____
C. I sometimes twist the truth to get what I want or to avoid getting hurt. _____
D. I listen more than I speak. _____

A. I am concerned about the plight of others _____

B. We are each responsible for our own situations. _____

C. I can persuade people to do what I want without them knowing it. _____
D. I value telling the truth over sparing the feelings of my friends. _____

Totals

Add the totals for each of the 10 As, 10 Bs, 10 Cs, and 10 Ds and enter the scores on the lines below.

A _____ B _____ C _____ D _____

The largest score indicates your primary tongue or communication style.

Tame Your Tongue and Transform Your Relationship

Interpreting Your Assessment Score

Please write your score for each section in the space provided. Your highest score indicates your *typical* communication style. It depicts the type of tongue with which you speak most often. Be sure to read about each of the four tongues in the pages that follow. Pay particular attention to your own.

Scores

A = the **Caring** tongue　　　　　　　_____

Those with this speech pattern speak truthfully while seeking to encourage.

B = the **Careless** tongue　　　　　　_____

Those with this speech pattern are filled with lies, curses, quick-tempered words which can lead to rebellion and destruction.

C = the **Conniving** tongue　　　　　_____

Those with this speech pattern are filled with wrong motives, gossip, slander, and a desire to twist truth.

D = the **Controlled** tongue　　　　　_____

Those with this speech pattern think before speaking, know when silence is best, and give wise advice.

We all have room to tame our tongues, especially if the caring tongue is not our typical style. As you continue to read, you will learn how your tongue may be speaking death into your relationships. Do not despair. This book will give you tips on how to tame your tongue.

Tame Your Tongue and Transform Your Relationship

Imagine the four tongues charted on a four quadrant grid as in Figure 1. The vertical axis, or dimension, measures the extent to which an individual talks. Are you someone who talks a lot or a little? Do you freely share information and speak what is on your mind? Or are you someone who thinks about what to say before carefully selecting what words to use? Would you prefer to listen rather than speak? The amount of talking that you engage in is one indication of your tongue.

The horizontal axis, or dimension, measures the degree of compassion that you express when speaking. Do you criticize, spread gossip, curse, or use profanity? Do you speak in evil ways with little, if any, caring? Do you say what is on your mind regardless of how it may make others feel? Or, are you known for being supportive and encouraging? Do you have something kind to say about everyone? If you use loving, encouraging words regardless of the circumstances you show great compassion in your speech. The amount of compassion reflected in your words is another indication of your tongue. Both indicators – the amount of talking you do and the level of compassion in your speech – are needed to determine your tongue.

An individual high on talking and high on compassion tends to speak a lot. She looks for opportunities to express her thoughts — not to uplift herself, but to strengthen someone else. Her words are loving and encouraging. She has a caring tongue.

In contrast, someone who is high on talking and low on compassion speaks a lot also, but her words are not as kind. She also looks for opportunities to express her thoughts, but she does not have the best interest of others in her heart or her mind. She only speaks highly of herself. When speaking of others, her words tend to include lies, malice, and discontent. She has a careless tongue.

If your speech pattern reflects little verbal expression, your tongue is either conniving or controlled. The conniving tongue is not only low on talking, but low on compassion, as well. A conniving person does not usually talk much. When she does, she thinks before she speaks. However, what she is thinking about is how to get what she wants. This may involve twisting the truth and manipulating the situation. It demonstrates a get-them-before-they-get-you mindset, characteristic of one who has been hurt or abused.

Last, but not least, is the controlled tongue. This person does not talk a lot. Because of her high compassion, she thinks before speaking so that her carefully chosen words do no harm, but are instead, comforting and wise.

Each of us is capable of speaking in any of these four tongues, and, on occasion, we utilize them all. We are likely to use them interchangeably depending on our mood or the situation. However, we have a natural propensity to utilize one of the four more than the

Tame Your Tongue and Transform Your Relationship

others; particularly in a situation where we react quickly and without thinking. I would encourage you to think about the best tongue to use before you speak. In doing so, remember that two of these four tongues are to be emulated while the other two are best avoided. God has given us free will to choose. Which tongue will you be known by? Which tongue will you choose?

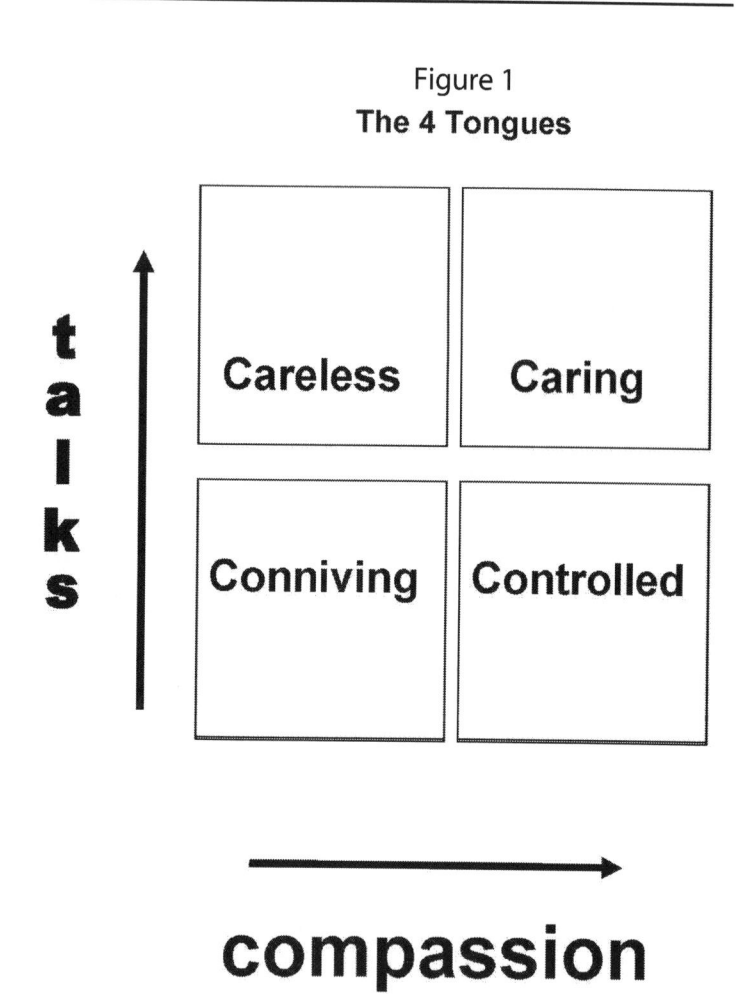

Figure 1
The 4 Tongues

talks ↑	Careless	Caring
	Conniving	Controlled

→ **compassion**

Tame Your Tongue and Transform Your Relationship

The 4 Tongues

Deceitful	Reckless	Prudent	Patient
Proud	Self-centered	Even tempered	Pleasant
Malicious	Gossiper	Wise	Gentle
Hypocritical	Dishonest	Guarded	Encouraging
CONNIVING	**CARELESS**	**CONTROLLED**	**CARING**

⬆ Compassion ⬆

Potential Impacts

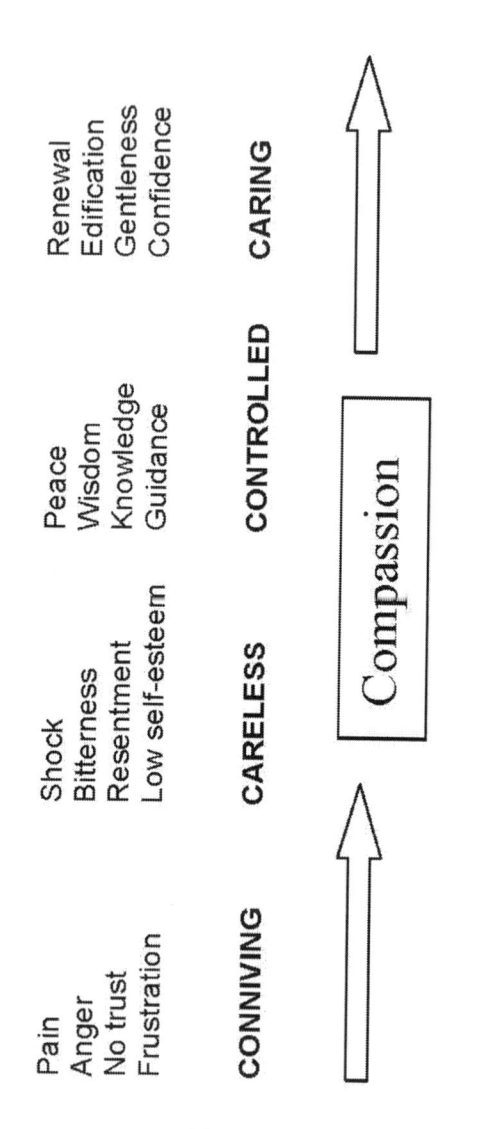

Pain	Shock	Peace	Renewal
Anger	Bitterness	Wisdom	Edification
No trust	Resentment	Knowledge	Gentleness
Frustration	Low self-esteem	Guidance	Confidence
CONNIVING	**CARELESS**	**CONTROLLED**	**CARING**

⇧ Compassion ⇧

The 4 Tongues in Action

Tame Your Tongue and Transform Your Relationship

Identifying your tongue in an assessment is one thing; identifying it in your daily routine requires much more skill and practice. Let's begin by first observing the tongues through the actions of others. The popular movie, *Deliver Us From Eva* shows how one woman is transformed from speaking with a conniving tongue to speaking with a caring tongue.

As the story goes, the four Dandridge sisters are smart, beautiful, and successful. When their parents are killed in a car accident, the oldest daughter Evangeline (Eva), at the young age of 18, assumes the responsibility of raising her three younger sisters. Eva takes this responsibility very seriously and let's nothing get in the way — not the love of her life or the romantic endeavors of her sisters. As a result, she develops a reputation of being, well ... let's just say, very hard core, insensitive, and unworthy of love. She cuts down every man around her with the sharpest tool known to mankind – the tongue.

Early in the movie, Eva demonstrates a conniving tongue in many ways. Here are two examples.

1. "I don't like getting in married people's business, but ... "

2. [To the Reverend regarding her sermon], "I took the liberty of jotting down a few suggestions of how you can do better in the future."

Wow! Does Eva have a hidden agenda or what? In both situations, she is trying to get what she wants in a "down-low" kind of way. With regard to the first statement, Eva's sister Kareena and her husband, Tim, are at odds over whether or not to have a baby. Tim is ready to start a family, but Kareena (due to Eva's influence) thinks they should wait. As Eva and Kareena discuss the situation, Eva meddles in their business . . . again. The comment is deceitful because the word "but" cancels out everything that precedes it. If Eva did not want to get into married people's business, she would just keep her mouth closed.

The conniving tongue believes she has all the answers. She knows best, and while she may not say that she is always right, you will probably never hear her admit that she is wrong. She knows how to be malicious while appearing to be ever-so charming. What a hypocrite! Eva's comment caused Kareena to doubt her own desires about starting a family. Tim became frustrated at the lack of leadership he was able to exhibit in his own home. The result was an environment of contention and bitter conflict; in a word, strife. When you find

Tame Your Tongue and Transform Your Relationship

strife in a relationship, it is a good indication that there may be a conniving tongue at work.

These characteristics are duplicated in Eva's statement about the reverend's sermon. Eva is very nit-picky about one word she believes the reverend omitted when quoting from the Bible. Consequently, Eva offers to help. What she is really doing is trying to impress the reverend with her knowledge of scripture. Eva's tongue has the potential to make the reverend feel attacked and, therefore, respond defensively. If such comments are repeated over time, they might weaken her confidence and minimize her ability to deliver a powerful sermon. Often, this is the intent of the conniving tongue. Because the conniving tongue believes she is always right, Eva believes she can improve upon the sermon of a minister. As usual, the conniving tongue is only focused on herself, therefore, she misses "the forest for the trees".

Eva's current and prospective brothers-in-law come up with a fool-proof plan. They hire the best player they know, Ray, to date Eva and distract her from interfering in their relationships. Ray is successful in getting Eva to go out with him. Eva demonstrates a careless tongue with statements such as:

1. "A messed up man is redundant"

2. "How does a meat delivery man afford a nice place like this?"

These statements are careless because a careless tongue says exactly what is on her mind, raw and uncut, regardless of how it may make others feel. Her statements are reckless and often exaggerated. The careless tongue has strong opinions and shares them with everyone within the sound of her voice. This is her "gift" to you whether you ask her or not. She does not think about ulterior motives. In fact, the problem is, she doesn't think at all. All she cares about is herself – what she thinks, what she wants, how she feels. People appear to befriend her when actually they just tolerate her in an attempt to avoid her sharp, cutting tongue. However, she is so caught up in herself that she doesn't even notice that she is being tolerated and not truly valued as a friend. Both of the statements above are examples of reckless, insensitive statements that are characteristic of a careless tongue.

As the story progresses, Eva is transformed. She allows herself to feel the love of a man who, by now, has genuine feelings for her. Isn't it amazing what love can do? Eva's heart is transformed and so is her tongue. "For out of the overflow of his heart his mouth speaks." (Luke 6:45) [NIV] She is no longer interested in manipulating the lives of others or hurting their feelings and their spirits. She no longer consistently speaks from a reckless place as she once did. Now, Eva clearly stops to consider the impact of her words before they leave her mouth. She exercises control over what she says. Eva is now interested in creating an aura of peace. An

Tame Your Tongue and Transform Your Relationship

example of statements she uses that demonstrate a controlled tongue are:

1. "Deal with whatever pain you have by building a bridge over it."

2. "I never had a guy who cared so much about my feelings."

These statements represent a controlled tongue because they reflect knowledge, wisdom, guidance, and peace.

Finally, by the end of the movie, Eva's entire disposition has changed. She is in a committed romantic relationship and she is in love. We can ask the proverbial chicken-or -egg question and ask if Eva's transformation led to her getting a man or if getting a man led to the transformation of her tongue. Either way, here are some examples of statements from a caring tongue.

1. "You taught me how to trust again."

2. "If you're going to be here then this is exactly where I want to be."

The caring tongue is pleasant and gentle. She uses words that are encouraging. They reflect the fact that she has been edified and renewed. The new Eva literally rode off with the man of her dreams. You can too. Before you go, let's look at each of the four tongues in more detail. You need to be able to recognize which tongue you are using every time you speak. I want you to know the characteristics of each tongue so that, if necessary, you can achieve your own personal communication style transformation. In other words, learn how to tame your tongue.

Tame Your Tongue and Transform Your Relationship

"Let all bitterness and wrath and anger and clamor and slander be put away from you, along with all malice. And be kind to one another, tender-hearted, forgiving each other, just as God in Christ also has forgiven you."
Ephesians 4:31-32

Chapter 3
The Conniving Tongue

It was November 10, a Saturday I believe, and I was buying a treadmill. Upon leaving the store, I was approached by a gentleman who wanted to talk to me. His name was "David" I was not attracted to him, but he seemed to be a nice guy. When I learned that he was saved and attended a well-known teaching church in the area, I gave him my number. Three days later he called. We met for coffee the next day and continued to get together for coffee or a meal for the next few weeks. A month later we were in a relationship and I still wasn't attracted to him – not physically anyway. David was not like most of the men I dated, which could be a good thing. He had most of the things on my checklist except the physical things. I didn't find his face very attractive and he was a little over-weight; not fat, just not lean and muscular. However, being the mature woman that I was, I knew that physical characteristics were not the most important factors to consider when choosing someone to date. Besides, I had ten extra pounds that I wanted to shed myself.

I thought I wanted a relationship with David. What I actually wanted was a relationship with the man that David could become. I began to subtly change him. Of course, I couldn't tell him that I didn't find him attractive, so I changed him with my conniving tongue. I described for David what I liked in a man. I liked "my man" to be fine (based on my definition of fine, of course), to have a nice body, lots of muscles, dress well, etc. I told him that I needed for "my man" to either have a fine face or a fine body, if not both. Then, I began suggesting that we go to the gym. (Now, David was no saint. He commented on my body, too). We set up a bet on who would reach his or her goals first. I knew that since he couldn't change his face (which really wasn't bad, just not what I wanted). He would have to change his body for us to be together. I found a way to get him to work on looking the way I wanted him to look and I did it in the name of "love." Isn't that awful?

But it didn't stop there. He owned five work outfits. Count them 1, 2, 3, 4. 5! He had to go to the cleaners every Friday. No matter where we were and what we were doing, he had to get to the cleaners by 6 PM on Saturday so he would have something to wear to work the following week. One of his work outfits was a grey, brushed cotton leisure suit that he wore with a shirt and tie! I was done! I said things like, "You know what would really look good on you?" and then inserted a suggestion of clothes he should buy. Or "Where do you buy your clothes?" I asked, "How do the people in your office dress?" When he would bring up career aspirations, I would mention the importance of dressing to impress. Obviously, looks were a

Tame Your Tongue and Transform Your Relationship

priority! Without realizing it, I was speaking to David with a conniving tongue.

The woman with a conniving tongue thinks before she speaks, but not to choose compassionate words or to keep from saying hurtful things. She thinks because she has a goal in mind and she needs to choose just the right words, tone, and timing to get what she wants. A very clever woman, she is so interested in getting her own way that she will say or do whatever it takes to make that happen. She will plan her approach for days just to be sure she gets all of the necessary factors into alignment. The words she uses may not be hurtful. She may not curse or use nasty language, but the actual words are not the only thing that makes her tongue conniving. It is the intent behind the words she chooses. The conniving tongue thinks of ways to manipulate the situation. She may not intend to be hurtful; she just wants what she wants. I didn't want to hurt David. I just wanted his appearance to be pleasing to me as if what I wanted was more important than what he wanted.

Some women know when they are using a conniving tongue, but others don't have a clue. Either way, the conniving tongue is deceitful. She doesn't come out and say what she wants for fear of being disliked or rejected. She manipulates people to get what she wants and she does it in a very charming way. She can make you think she is doing something for your benefit when all the while she is scheming for herself. For some women this is sport. It's like a game to them to see how well they can "play" other people. Other women speak with a conniving tongue because they are controlling by nature. They want to direct the outcome of every situation and they use their tongues as a tool in the process.

The conniving tongue will sometimes take deceit to the level of lying. A lying tongue indicates hatred in the heart. It may be hatred for the individual she is speaking to, or hatred towards some specific aspect of that person's behavior or personality. Sometimes the hatred is directed at people that the individual represents to her. For example, maybe her boyfriend is arrogant which reminds her of her boss. Since she cannot lash out at her boss, she lashes out at her boyfriend. Sometimes a conniving tongue is created out of self-hatred. Many people have internalized the bad things that have happened to them. They come to believe that they are not worthy of love and respect since people they cared for did not love and respect them. Part of the way they show their disdain for self is by attacking others. It keeps people from getting close to them and caring about them which, in turn, reinforces the belief that they are unworthy.

The devil gets us to sabotage ourselves by getting a hold of our tongues. If he can get our tongues then he can get the rest of us. All he has to do is get us to contradict the truth which is found in God's Word. The truth according to the Word says, "By [Jesus's] stripes ye were healed..." (1 Peter 2:24) [KJV]. When we say, "I'm just so sick!" We are lying. We are giving the devil a foothold into

Tame Your Tongue and Transform Your Relationship

our lives, and setting the course for a life full of sickness. We don't become sick because we said it, but we do give in to sickness if we begin to feel ill. We lose energy and motivation because those things coincide with being well and we have developed a mindset of being sick.

The devil uses our tongue to say "I am so broke!" Again, this is not a prophetic statement, but we start concentrating on what we lack rather than what we have. We see obstacles instead of opportunities. As a result, we don't see the possibilities that lie before us. But Christ said He came that we might have life and have it more abundantly. If we say anything other than what the Word of God says about a situation, we are lying against the truth and deceiving ourselves.

It's not too surprising, then, that when we feel under pressure or overwhelmed in some way, we tend to open our mouths and say things like, "I'm so unworthy!" "I'm so tired!" "I'm so broke!" "I'm so ugly!" "I'm never going anywhere in life!" You see, sometimes when we speak with a conniving tongue we lie on ourselves. When the pressure is on, that's when we really find out what's on the inside of us - and it's usually not the Word of God.

"Be careful how you think; your life is shaped by your thoughts." (Proverbs4:2) [Good News Version]

The conniving tongue gossips and gets involved in conversations that are not edifying. What is gossip?

Let's see: telling Karen" about Lynn's cheating husband; asking Carol if she heard about Beth's divorce; questioning how "Lisa" can afford that new car. When you talk to one friend about the personal business of another, even if what you are saying is true, that is gossip. The conniving tongue engages in conversations that are destructive and she believes she has done no harm! When you confront her about it, she denies it. She might even get tears in her eyes and say sorrowfully, "I'm not like that. Yes, I may have said some things that could be construed as gossip or careless. But God knows my heart. I never meant any harm."

What is the harm in "sharing" information about others? Everybody does it. That type of attitude is dangerous! The Bible says great fires are caused by little sparks! (James 3:5) And your little spark can ignite a big fire, even though you don't mean for it to get out of hand. You can nonchalantly drop a tidbit about somebody, and it can end up affecting their character, their spirit, and their relationships! It doesn't matter what your motive was — the damage is done. Your little spark has already started a fire, and it's raging out of control. It could damage a reputation. It may bring someone shame, disgrace and sorrow. And no matter what your motive was in telling it, you are still guilty - you are the fire bug! It was your unruly tongue that started it all!

The conniving tongue is proud. She possesses an unreasonable and inordinate self-esteem which causes her to become upset when things fall below her standards. As a result, she is always trying to help or fix some poor unfortunate soul. Her motives are all wrong. Proud people seldom realize that pride is their problem, although everyone around them is aware of it. Ask someone you trust if pride is one of your issues. Their response may help you avoid a fall.

Characteristics of a conniving tongue:
- Deceitful
- Proud and arrogant
- Gossip
- Hypocritical
- Charming
- Desire to impress
- Malicious

<u>The potential impact of the conniving tongue</u>. Whenever verbal communication takes place, the sender of the message (in this case the conniving tongue) has the power of creating a potential impact on the receiver of the message, (your man or woman), and therefore, on the relationship. If you speak to your man with a conniving tongue, you may be accused of being verbally or emotionally abusive. You may get your way, but you will find that the cost of getting your way is far greater than the benefit you expected. When people feel that their opinion doesn't matter, or even worse, that they don't matter, they begin to withdraw. Eventually, he will become frustrated and possibly angry.

When this happens, say good-bye to the trust you once shared. If you feel lonely and disconnected from your man, he may be withdrawing from you and it may be due to your conniving tongue.

Being totally consumed with the thought of gaining status, control, or power may result in you being the winner, but what did you win? The more powerfull you feel, the more power-less he feels. Have you noticed that he spends a lot of time with his friends, watching TV, reading the paper, or just away from the house altogether? What did you win if the two of you are not spending time together? At this rate, you may become a lonely, isolated person with few close relationships and many hidden enemies.

You may have experienced things in life that developed in you a conniving tongue. However, God is a God "who redeems your life from the pit and crowns you with love and compassion." (Psalm 103:4) [NIV] That same compassion that God gave to you is in you to give to another.

In chapter 8, you will read detailed instructions on how to tame your tongue. Here are a few quick tips.

How to tame a conniving tongue

- A lie is a weapon. Lying is vicious. Its effects can be as permanent as those of a stab wound. The next time you are tempted to

Tame Your Tongue and Transform Your Relationship

lie against the Word or pass on a bit of gossip, imagine yourself stabbing the victim of your remarks with a sword. This image may shock you into silence.

- Purify your heart by making a clean break with sin and committing yourself completely to God.

- Practice not being hypocritical: praising God one moment, while being careless with your words the next.

We like control, and that's okay, but we need to change the object of our control. Instead of controlling others with our tongues, we need to learn to control our own flesh. Control the things you say. In other words, tame your tongue and transform your relationship.

Reflections

1) A time when I spoke with this tongue was _____

_____

_____

_____

2) Some of the factors that led to this situation were

_____

_____

_____

3) Speaking with this tongue left me feeling _____

_____

_____

4) Speaking with this tongue left those around me feeling

_____

_____

Tame Your Tongue and Transform Your Relationship

5) To avoid speaking death into that relationship, I should have

_____

_____

_____

Meditation Scriptures
Proverbs (Good News Version)

6:12 Worthless, wicked people go around telling lies.

6:13 They wink and make gestures to deceive you,

6:14 all the while planning evil in their perverted minds, stirring up trouble everywhere.

8:13 To honor the Lord is to hate evil; I hate pride and arrogance, evil ways and false words.

16:28 Gossip is spread by wicked people; they stir up trouble and break up friendships.

18:8 The words of a gossip are like choice morsels; they go down to a man's inmost parts. (NIV)

25:18 A false accusation is as deadly as a sword, a club, or a sharp arrow.

26:20 Without wood a fire goes out; without gossip, quarreling stops.

26:21 Charcoal keeps the embers glowing, wood keeps the fire burning, and troublemakers keep arguments alive..

Tame Your Tongue and Transform Your Relationship

26:23   Insincere talk that hides what you are really thinking is like a fine glaze on a cheap clay pot.

26:24   A hypocrite hides hate behind flattering words

26:25   They may sound fine, but don't believe him, because his heart is filled to the brim with hate.

26:26   He may disguise his hatred, but everyone will see the evil things he does.

26:27   People who set traps for others get caught themselves. People who start landslides get crushed.

26:28   You have to hate someone to want to hurt him with lies. Insincere talk brings nothing but ruin.

Dr. Linda G. Wiley

"What dainty morsels rumors are – but they sink deep into one's heart."
Proverbs 18:8 (NLT)

Chapter 4
The Careless Tongue

Cheryl was upset! It was New Year's Eve and she had no place to go. She was in town visiting relatives for the holidays. It was the first time she had seen all of her aunts, uncles, and cousins in a long time. The family camaraderie had been great. It was an exciting time for a number of reasons. All week she anticipated going with her cousin Lance and some friends to the gospel comedy show for their New Year's Eve celebration. Cheryl and Lance had always been very close.

"Lance, do you have the tickets?" she would ask her cousin almost every day. "It's all under control," was the constant reply from Lance. Tonight, like clockwork, Cheryl called Lance to ask about the tickets. "Vicki is working with her Mom to get the tickets," was the reply from Lance. So Cheryl called her girls and they finalized their plans. She bought a new outfit, had her hair and nails done, and anxiously awaited the day and the hour.

Finally, it was New Year's Eve. Cheryl, her father, and grandmother were sitting in her aunt's family room after a fabulous dinner. Then, hours before the show, she got the bad news. Lance's girlfriend, Vicki, only bought two tickets — one for her and one for Lance. The show was sold out. Vicki and her mother had been trying all week to get tickets from a "reliable source," but to no avail. Cheryl and her friends would not be able to go.

"I don't believe him!" she raved as she paraded through the kitchen. All other conversations stopped and, as usual, everyone's attention was diverted to Cheryl. "I'm family! How dare he leave me out! He would rather go to the concert with that b—h than me. She's not even good enough to lick my boots! What am I supposed to do tonight? What am I supposed to tell my friends? I will NEVER speak to him again!"

Cheryl's comments after receiving the bad news are an example of someone speaking with a careless tongue. The woman who speaks with a careless tongue is one who speaks without thinking. Her lack of forethought results in comments that are reckless. She is never at a loss for words; unfortunately, her words are usually sarcastic or unkind. Someone with a careless tongue talks a lot. She's the kind of person that people say "runs off at the mouth." She is often seen as the life of the party and the center of attention, which is exactly what she wants. The careless tongue is so hungry for attention she would rather have negative attention than no attention at all.

Someone with a careless tongue says exactly what is on her mind without thinking about the impact her words may have on "the other guy." Saying what she thinks can be a good thing because you always

Tame Your Tongue and Transform Your Relationship

know where she is coming from. The problem, however, is that the careless tongue is low on compassion and truth without compassion is brutality.

The careless tongue is self-centered which prevents her from remembering that others have feelings and that those feelings are equally as important as her own. This perspective leads her to hurt others with her words. In fact, sometimes she speaks just so that she can be hurtful. She doesn't care who is in earshot and will often exaggerate things in order to draw attention to her plight.

The careless tongue is opinionated. She is usually full of energy and conversation. Pay attention and you will find that the theme of the conversation is herself — what she did, what she has, what she thinks, what she likes. Her conversation about other people usually portrays them in an unflattering manner. The careless tongue is no stranger to criticizing people in some way. Often the careless tongue spews lies and exaggerations or, at the least, information that she has not observed and cannot verify. It just sounds good at the moment while she is trying to make her point. Willona Woods (*Good Times*), Florence the maid (*The Jeffersons*), Nikki Parker (*The Parkers*), Toni Childs (*Girlfriends*), and Ma'Dea all have careless tongues. I occasionally *had* a careless tongue.

It was okay for Cheryl to be hurt and upset under the circumstances. What was not okay was her reaction

Dr. Linda G. Wiley

to the hurt that she was experiencing. She never once stopped to ask why there were only two tickets. Were any other tickets available? Were she and the others left out intentionally? Were there any other options? Instead of thinking only of herself, she could have called the other friends who did not get tickets to see about making alternate plans. She should have wished her cousin and his girlfriend a good time. And what about calling the girlfriend the "b" word? What's up with that? Putting others down never puts you ahead. It only makes you look bad.

The mouth can be used as a weapon or a tool, hurting relationships or building them up. Sadly, it is often easier to destroy than to build, and most people have received more destructive comments than those that build up. Every person you meet today is either a demolition site or a construction opportunity. Your words will determine the difference. Will they be weapons for destruction or tools for construction? Think before you speak. Don't let your emotions get the best of you. Calm down before you speak so you don't over react. When someone annoys or insults you, it is natural to want to retaliate. But this solves nothing and only encourages trouble. Instead, answer slowly and quietly. Your positive response will achieve positive results.

"A gentle answer turns away wrath." (Proverbs 15:1) [NIV]

Tame Your Tongue and Transform Your Relationship

Words can build barriers. Unless you become more careful and controlled with your tongue, you will find people developing emotional barriers in their relationships with you so that they are no longer vulnerable to being hurt. A person with a careless tongue risks being emotionally and verbally abusive in her dealings with others. The cost of always getting her way becomes greater than expected and often leads to loneliness and feeling disconnected from others.

A loose tongue renders all religion absolutely worthless! It can make your every spiritual activity totally useless in God's eyes: "If any one among you thinks he is religious, and does not bridle his tongue but deceives his own heart, this one's religion is useless." (James 1:26) [NIV]. James is speaking here of those "among you"—- that is, in the church. These aren't drug addicts or street people — they are part of the body of Christ who appear pious and spiritual. They are active in the work of the Lord. But their tongues are unbridled, out of control! James is zeroing in on those who seem to be holy, kind, gentle, loving - yet who move about the church or on their job or in their family with acid tongues, always listening to and telling morsels of gossip. They think nothing of murmuring and complaining. God says their religion - all their show of spirituality - is in vain. It's valueless, worthless!

Characteristics of a careless tongue:
- Speaking without thinking
- Recklessness
- Saying exactly what is on her mind – raw and uncut
- Self-centeredness
- Insensitive to the feelings of others
- Likes attention
- Opinionated
- Energetic
- Exaggerates
- Gossips

<u>The potential impact of the careless tongue</u>. Whenever verbal communication takes place, the sender of the message, (in this case the careless tongue), has the power of creating a potential impact on the receiver of the message, (your man or woman), and, therefore, on the relationship. If you speak to your man with a careless tongue, you may be getting bitterness and resentment in return. I'm not saying that you hooked up with a bitter person. I'm saying that all of that neck-rolling, finger-snapping, give-you-a-piece-of-my-mind stuff is creating animosity.

He doesn't appreciate your attitude or your tone and he will do just about anything to get away from you and your tongue. He doesn't mind listening to you, he just resents hearing about other people's problems and

Tame Your Tongue and Transform Your Relationship

your discontent. I know you are a diva, but can you share the spotlight every once in a while? If you always state your opinion and never ask him for his, you are building a wall between the two of you. Men need to be needed. That is one of the ways in which they measure the value that they bring to a relationship. He can't feel needed if he feels emasculated and the quickest way to strip him of his power is to beat him to death with your tongue. Your put downs are really push outs because you are pushing him right out of your life. Even if he doesn't physically leave the relationship, he will check out on you emotionally and sexually. The first woman who comes along and helps him find the self-esteem that you took will have a good chance of stealing his heart.

In chapter 8, you will read detailed instructions on how to tame your tongue. Here are a few quick tips.

<u>How to tame a careless tongue?</u>

- Choose your words carefully because they can have a long lasting, hurtful impact. You can negatively impact someone's self esteem and motivation by saying the wrong thing.

- Don't bring up past offenses. Try not to bring anything into an argument that is un-related to the topic being discussed. Argumentative words (and spirits) start small and then overflow. When you love to argue, you have a love of sin.

- Don't strike back with your words; let it go. Words are irretrievable. The story is told of a person who hurt an acquaintance very deeply by his words. In time he apologized. The friend forgave, but sought to impress the consequences of the harmful words. Taking a feather pillow, he went to the window and emptied its contents into the wind. Turning to the offender he said, "I forgive you, but you will no more be able to recover the harm done by your words than you are able to recover all those feathers."

Tame Your Tongue and Transform Your Relationship

Reflections

1) A time when I spoke with this tongue was _____

   _____

   _____

   _____

2) Some of the factors that led to this situation were

   _____

   _____

   _____

3) Speaking with this tongue left me feeling _____

   _____

   _____

4) Speaking with this tongue left those around me feeling

   _____

   _____

5) To avoid speaking death into that relationship, I should have

_____

_____

_____

Tame Your Tongue and Transform Your Relationship

<u>Meditation Scriptures</u>
<u>Proverbs</u> (Good News Version)

10:18   Anyone who hides hatred is a liar. Anyone who spreads gossip is a fool.

10:32   Righteous people know the kind thing to say, but the wicked are always saying things that hurt.

11:9   You can be ruined by the talk of godless people, but the wisdom of the righteous can save you.

12:16   When a fool is annoyed, he quickly lets it be known. Smart people will ignore an insult.

12:18   Reckless words pierce like a sword, but the tongue of the wise brings healing. (NIV)

15:4   Kind words bring life, but cruel words crush your spirit.

17:9   If you want people to like you, forgive them when they wrong you. Remembering wrongs can break up a friendship.

17:14   The start of an argument is like the first break in a dam; stop it before it goes any further.

17:19 To like sin is to like making trouble. If you brag all the time, you are asking for trouble.

20:19 A gossip can never keep a secret. Stay away from people who talk too much.

25:23 Gossip brings anger just as surely as the north wind brings rain.

Tame Your Tongue and Transform Your Relationship

"This you know, my beloved brethren. But let everyone be quick to hear, slow to speak and slow to anger; for the anger of man does not achieve the righteousness of God."
James 1:19-20

Chapter 5
The Controlled Tongue

Every day we can hear untamed tongues in action filling the world with damaging criticism, slander, sarcasm, maligning, gossip, exaggerations, distortions, innuendos and blasphemies. The psalmist spoke of the need of bringing the tongue under God's control: "Set a guard over my mouth, O LORD; keep watch over the door of my lips." (Psalm 141:3) [NIV]

According to the <u>American Heritage Dictionary</u>, the word "control" means
1. To adjust to a requirement; regulate
2. To hold in restraint; check
3. To reduce or prevent the spread of
4. A standard of comparison for checking or verifying the results of an experiment.

What would happen if things weren't regulated? You know, things like gas prices, insurance rates, and airline safety. What would happen if there was no way to hold certain entities in check? Things like crowds, loud noises, large bodies of water. Can you imagine what

Dr. Linda G. Wiley

the world would be like if we had no way to reduce the spread of certain diseases? There would be epidemics of smallpox, AIDS, bird flu, and God only knows what else

When we hear the word "control" or "controlled," we tend to think that some outside force will restrain or direct us like in "government control." We believe that we will be giving up or losing power to someone else. By nature, we don't like to be controlled. We want to be free to think and do as we please without having to answer to anyone.

From a biblical perspective, control involves giving up our own power to the One who holds all power. As believers, that is how we are to live every day. God gave us control over our lives in the form of free will. Then, He asked us to submit and joyfully give our will back to Him.

The woman who speaks with a controlled tongue recognizes that it is out of our freedom that we control ourselves. She takes the locus of control (or perception of where control comes from), away from an external source and places it internally, on herself. She takes control over the words that flow from her mouth. The more she talks, the more room there is for the sin that is in her (and in all of us) to enter into her thoughts and her words. Therefore, it is best to say little in certain situations. Bottom line: We just need to say less! Proverbs 17:27-28 says, "A man of knowledge uses words with restraint...even a fool is thought wise if he keeps silent, and discerning if he holds his tongue."

The controlled tongue is even-tempered. She has emotions, but is not quick to show them, especially if they are negative. Being a woman of compassion, she would not want to make others feel bad. When she is hurt or offended, she resists the natural inclination to retaliate because she knows that it accomplishes nothing and encourages trouble. Therefore, by grace and forgiveness the controlled tongue overlooks insults. Her attitude is contagious and by not over-reacting, her behavior helps others to do the same. She is the kind of person who strives to always have a nice day.

The controlled tongue will not be the most talkative one at the party. She will probably sit back as others speak. She recognizes that there are benefits to keeping quiet. That type of posture allows her the opportunity to listen and learn, so she will do a great deal of listening.

Because she is wise, she makes prudent use of her words. Unlike the careless tongue, the controlled tongue rarely speaks without thinking. However, her thinking is not for the purpose of manipulating the situation and getting her own way. She takes the time to choose just the right words that convey her thoughts *and* do no harm. She is concerned about how her words will make others feel. Some may say she is guarded just as King David asked God to guard his mouth (Psalm 141:3).

Dr. Linda G. Wiley

It was the Friday before the 4th of July holiday. My oldest son and I had appointments with our ophthalmologist. As soon as we arrived at the doctor's office my cell phone rang. You see, we were having trouble with the air conditioning unit that controlled the air upstairs. It was summertime in Georgia and it was impossible to sleep in that heat. We had been dealing with the situation for about two weeks. This was the third time the company was sending out a technician. Under the circumstances, I felt I had to leave and go home to let in the technician.

On my way back to the ophthalmologist's office, an 18 year old boy rear-ended my new Lexus SC 430 convertible. I loved that car as soon as it came out, but, I waited a few years before buying it. I wanted to be sure I could afford it. I wanted to be able to buy it guilt-free. Then, I searched the internet for just the right one. A friend negotiated a sweet deal for me. Another friend flew with me from Georgia to Ohio to pick up the car and drive it back home. Can you feel what this car meant to me? In addition to all of that, the car was so new it did not even have the permanent license plate on it yet.

I think anyone, no, everyone, would have understood if I became livid. Who would have faulted me for ranting and raving? However, I saw the look of fear and remorse on that young man's face and I was not the least bit angry. I found myself saying, "It's okay. I know you are sorry, but don't worry about it. We're not hurt. The car is a material thing and material things can be replaced." That, my friends, was a controlled tongue (with a little caring thrown in). I chose to put myself in that young man's place and show him the *compassion that I would want to feel. It would have been so easy to yell at him since he was clearly at fault. But I have a son about his age and I would certainly want someone to have compassion on my son if he were in that situation.*

The controlled tongue has a sense of peace about her. That peace permeates throughout her relationships and helps to keep everyone else calm. It's hard to argue with someone who speaks gently. She is guided by the Word of God. That is the standard that she upholds. When she speaks she educates others on how they also can meet God's standard.

Characteristics of a controlled tongue:
- Prudent
- Understanding
- Discerning of when to speak
- Trustworthy
- Somewhat guarded
- Wise and instructive
- Even-tempered

<u>The potential impact of the controlled tongue</u>. Whenever verbal communication takes place, the sender of the message (in this case the controlled tongue) has the power of creating a potential impact on the receiver of the message, (your man or woman), and therefore on the relationship. If you speak to your man with a controlled tongue, you are helping the relationship to

grow. When you speak in an even-tempered way you increase the likelihood that he will listen and hear you. Why? Because he feels talked *to*, not talked *at*. The relationship grows because the controlled tongue takes time to think before speaking. She takes a moment to consider what she intends to say and the impact that her words will have. Calm down, choose your words wisely, then speak. Your carefully chosen words will reflect an understanding, or at least an attempt to understand the situation and the feelings that ensue.

Trust develops in the relationship because your partner can count on you to keep your emotions under control. Therefore, the message comes through with less noise. Feedback is allowed. In other words, he can ask clarifying questions and feel free to contribute to the dialogue. The controlled tongue imparts wisdom and creates an atmosphere of peace.

In chapter 8, you will read detailed instructions on how to tame your tongue. Here are a few quick tips.

<u>How to develop a controlled tongue</u>

- Practice listening instead of speaking.
- Too much talking can get you in trouble. When you don't have anything of value to say, say nothing.
- Let love and compassion guide your words and use your words to teach.

Tame Your Tongue and Transform Your Relationship

Reflections

1) A time when I spoke with this tongue was _____

   _____

   _____

   _____

2) Some of the factors that led to this situation were

   _____

   _____

   _____

3) Speaking with this tongue left me feeling _____

   _____

   _____

4) Speaking with this tongue left those around me feeling

   _____

   _____

5) To avoid speaking death into that relationship, I should have

_____

_____

_____

Tame Your Tongue and Transform Your Relationship

<u>Meditation Scriptures</u>
<u>Proverbs</u> (Good News Version)

10:19   The more you talk, the more likely you are to sin. If you are wise, you will keep quiet.

11:12   It is foolish to speak scornfully of others. If you are smart, you will keep quiet.

11:13   No one who gossips can be trusted with a secret, but you can put confidence in someone who is trustworthy.

12:16   When a fool is annoyed, he quickly lets it be known. Smart people will ignore an insult.

13:3   Be careful what you say and protect your life. A careless talker destroys himself.

15:1   A gentle answer quiets anger, but a harsh one stirs it up.

15:4   Kind words bring life, but cruel words crush your spirit.

15:28   Good people think before they answer. Evil people have a quick reply, but it causes trouble.

16:23   Intelligent people think before they speak; what they say is then more persuasive.

17:14 The start of an argument is like the first break in a dam; stop it before it goes any further.

17:27 Those who are sure of themselves do not talk all the time. People who stay calm have real insight.

17:28 After all, even fools may be thought wise and intelligent if they stay quiet and keep their mouths shut.

21:23 If you want to stay out of trouble, be careful what you say.

24:26 An honest answer is a sign of true friendship.

Tame Your Tongue and Transform Your Relationship

"Pleasant words are a honeycomb, sweet to the
soul and healing to the bones."
Proverbs 16:24, NIV

Chapter 6
The Caring Tongue

Have you ever planted a flower garden? If you have, you know that tools are a very important part of the process. They are useful in removing rocks, tree stumps, and other debris that might be in the way. Gardening tools are needed to level and aerate the soil and to bring in additional soil, mix in the fertilizer, etc.

One of the most essential tools for any gardener, new or experienced, is a small, handheld shovel called a dowel. On a very small scale, the dowel can be used to perform any of the tasks listed above. It can be used to move debris (no tree stumps of course), move soil, and so on. The dowel is best known for digging holes. You see, before you can plant a seed, a seedling, or a bulb, there must first be a hole in the soil. So the gardener, dowel in hand, digs a hole just the right size to plant this new life that will grow. The dowel is a tool quite often used in projects of growth and building up.

Ironically, if you want to uproot and dismantle the plant, bringing its vitality to an end, the dowel is also useful. The dowel has a pointed end that is sharp and cuts deep. When plunged into the soil, the dowel scoops it up and destroys the roots that held the plant

Dr. Linda G. Wiley

in place. Once the root is destroyed, the plant can no longer be nourished and it begins to die. The dowel is a tool that the gardener can use to build or to destroy. The tongue is a tool, also, and like the dowel, can be used to build or to destroy.

The caring tongue shows compassion. They use words to soothe, comfort, and heal. When you speak with a caring tongue, you find the right words to say. Scripture says, "The lips of the righteous know what is fitting, but the mouth of the wicked only what is perverse." (Proverbs 10:32) [NIV] When we feel compassion or love for someone, we have a tendency to want to help them grow into their full potential and flourish. We communicate with them frequently. We choose our words carefully so that we express even our negative thoughts and emotions in a non-offensive way. When we feel compassion or love for someone, we tell them things they need to hear and we give them advice. Their best interest is in our hearts and we focus on their well-being. We have a desire to encourage them with the truth because care and concern is on our hearts. In this situation, the tongue is caring because the tongue reveals the heart.

The caring tongue is not deceitful. She is genuine and honest. The caring tongue is not proud and arrogant. She is humble and non-assuming. The caring tongue is not a gossip. She tells stories that educate and edify. The caring tongue is not a hypocrite. She is a woman of integrity. The caring tongue is not seeking to impress others. She is more concerned about their welfare. The caring tongue is not reckless. She thinks before she speaks to find the right words to heal and uplift.

The woman who speaks with a caring tongue is pleasant and encouraging. She is not focused solely on herself and has concern for feelings other than her own. If Cheryl used a caring tongue when she spoke to Lance, she may have said something like this:

> *"Well, Lance, I am a little disappointed, but I'm sure you did your best to get the tickets as you said you would. Do you know what happened? I would like to explain the situation to my friends. Do you have any suggestions for something else we can do tonight to bring in the new year? Well, I am going to try to put it behind me and you should too. Go out and have a good time. Oh yeah, happy new year!"*

What if I had chosen to be caring with David? Instead of focusing on what he lacked, I should have focused on what he brought to the table. Remember, I said he had most of the qualities on my compatibility shopping list. On paper, he was a good man for me. If I chose to speak with a caring tongue, I would have complimented him on all of the good qualities he possessed. The potential impact would have been a man who felt so good about himself and about us, that he would have looked for other ways to please me and receive my praise. (Actually, David had other issues that led to our break-up, but you get the idea). He would have chosen to lose weight for himself. And if he didn't, so what? Would I be better off with a man who treated me well but did not have an extensive, stylish wardrobe or vice versa?

When you use your words to encourage someone else's life, the results bring you joy as well. Just as using your dowel to work as a tool for growth, you and everyone around you benefits from the beautiful flowers that grow. True joy comes not from uplifting yourself or focusing on your own strengths and achievements, but from focusing on the strengths and achievements of others. The person with the caring tongue is like the gardener who plants. Her words will lead to a harvest that nourishes life. Everyone wants to be loved. The caring tongue is wise enough to know that the object of love is not *getting* something you want but *doing* something for the well-being of the one you love. It has been demonstrated that when we receive affirming words we are far more motivated to speak affirming words than if they were not spoken to us.

"This is what the Lord Almighty says: 'Administer true justice; show mercy and compassion to one another." (Zechariah 7:9) [NIV]

"Be kind and compassionate to one another, forgiving each other, just as in Christ God forgave you." (Ephesians 4:32) [NIV]

Tame Your Tongue and Transform Your Relationship

"Therefore, as God's chosen people, holy and dearly loved, clothe yourselves with compassion, kindness, humility, gentleness and patience." (Colossians 3:12) [NIV]

Characteristics of a caring tongue:
- Knows what to say and when
- Wisdom
- Kindness
- Pleasantness
- Patience
- Gentleness
- Understanding

<u>The potential impact of the caring tongue</u>. Whenever verbal communication takes place, the sender of the message (in this case the caring tongue) has the power of creating a potential impact on the receiver of the message (your man or woman), and therefore on the relationship. If you speak to your man with a caring tongue, you speak life into your relationship. The patience and gentleness of the caring tongue lets your mate know that you care about him. Your kindness is likely to be met with kindness. He doesn't run from you; he runs towards you. Because you express the desire to genuinely understand him and his feelings, he takes the time to share them with you.

The atmosphere created by the caring tongue is a breeding ground for confidence. When someone feels confident, especially confident in their relationship, there is no need to ask a lot of questions about where you are going, who you are talking to, how much you are spending. Those questions represent the conversation of the insecure. Because the caring tongue edifies and renews, every day is fresh and new. The caring tongue is the one that you can't wait to get home to.

How do you develop a caring tongue? Read on!

Tame Your Tongue and Transform Your Relationship

Reflections

1) A time when I spoke with this tongue was _____

_____

_____

_____

2) Some of the factors that led to this situation were

_____

_____

_____

3) Speaking with this tongue left me feeling _____

_____

_____

4) Speaking with this tongue left those around me feeling

_____

_____

5) To avoid speaking death into that relationship, I should have

_____

_____

_____

Tame Your Tongue and Transform Your Relationship

<u>Meditation Scriptures</u>
<u>Proverbs</u> (Good News Version)

10:32   Righteous people know the kind thing to say, but the wicked are always saying things that hurt.

12:18   Thoughtless words can wound as deeply as any sword, but wisely spoken words can heal.

12:25   Worry can rob you of happiness, but kind words will cheer you up.

15:23   What a joy it is to find just the right word for the right occasion!

16:24   Kind words are like honey – sweet to the taste and good for your health.

25:15   Patient persuasion can break down the strongest resistance and can even convince rulers.

27:9   Perfume and fragrant oils make you feel happier, but trouble shatters your peace of mind.

Chapter 7
Why Tame Your Tongue?

"The tongue has the power of life and death,"
Proverbs 18:21a (NIV)

We all make mistakes. But if a person never makes a mistake in what he says, he is perfect and is also able to control his whole being. We put a bit into the mouth of a horse to make it obey us, and we are able to make it go where we want. Or think of a ship: big as it is and driven by such strong winds, it can be steered by a very small rudder, and it goes wherever the pilot wants it to go. So it is with the tongue: small as it is, it can boast about great things.

Just think how a large forest can be set on fire by a tiny flame! And the tongue is like a fire. It is a world of wrong, occupying its place in our bodies and spreading evil through our whole being. It sets on fire the entire course of our existence with the fire that comes to it from hell itself. We humans are able to tame and have tamed all other creatures – wild animals and birds, reptiles and fish. But no one has ever been able to tame the tongue. It is evil and uncontrollable, full of deadly poison. We use it to give thanks to our Lord and Father and also to cure other people, who are created in the likeness of God. Words of thanksgiving and cursing pour out from the same mouth. My friends, this should not happen! No spring of water pours out sweet water and bitter water from the same opening. A fig tree, my friends, cannot bear olives; a grapevine cannot bear figs, nor can a salty spring produce sweet water." (James 3:2-12) [Good News Version]

These words were written by James, the brother of Jesus, somewhere around A.D. 49. He was writing to first-century Jewish Christians and all Christians everywhere. The purpose of the letter was to expose hypocritical practices and to teach Christians the right way to behave. James starts out by keeping it real. He lets us know right away that we all make mistakes with what we say. The only person who doesn't make such mistakes is perfect and none of us is perfect. He makes a connection between what we say and our whole being. What we harbor inside of us comes out of our mouths and what we speak affects our whole being. It is like the bit that gives the horse direction. Our tongues give direction to our lives. If we speak with a tongue that is careless or conniving, we will reap the consequences of being careless or conniving. Likewise, if we speak with a tongue that is controlled or caring, we will reap the benefits of being controlled or caring. One reason to tame the tongue is to have better control over our whole self.

James leaves no question as to the power we hold in our tongues. That power can either work for us or it can work against us. Every time we open our mouths to speak,

Tame Your Tongue and Transform Your Relationship

we are the ones who decide. You may think that the conniving tongue works for you because, for the moment, you get your way. But, what about the long-term health of the relationship? What about God's judgment? Jesus said in Matthew 12:3, "Your words will be used to judge you – to declare you either innocent or guilty." If you are found innocent, you may be in position to receive God's favor; if found guilty, probably not. So another reason to tame the tongue is because it will be used to judge you.

There is no storm on life's sea through which we cannot safely sail by proper use of the rudder that is in our mouths. Our tongues can be a powerful tool used in our favor. They can also be an unruly and deadly force, causing our lives to be shipwrecked if we let them run out of control. Our only hope for taming our tongues, and thereby charting a good course for our future, is through the power of the Holy Spirit. "But no man can tame the tongue." (James 3:8a, NIV).

The tongue you choose when you speak is critical to harmonious relationships. As you learn to speak the truth in love, you must also determine when to speak and how to speak in an edifying manner. The power of your words is enormous and they show the condition of your heart. Since none of us is perfect in any way, we all stumble with our speech. We can all benefit from improving the effectiveness of how we speak to others.

Our words go before us. We formulate opinions about others based, in part, on what they say. If a man

approaches you with a pick-up line like, "Don't I know you from somewhere?" or "Girl, you look good. Can I holla at you for a minute?" What impression does he make? I'll tell you. You will probably think one of the following:
- How lame!
- I am not about to waste my time with this one
- He's not the most creative individual I've ever met

Your expectations of him will not be very high. And when you tell your girls about him (and you know you will), you will talk about his opening line and little else. Why? Because once he hits you with that profound introduction, you won't hear anything else that he says. If you respond in one of the ways described above, your response will be conniving. He may be lame, but you will be conniving. As we've seen, the conniving tongue is very judgmental. It gossips with mal-intent. You will be guilty of putting him down in an effort to boost yourself up. Words reveal a lot about who we are and how we think. That's why we need to choose them carefully.

A third reason to tame your tongue is because your words are a mirror of your heart. Our speech and actions reveal our true underlying beliefs, attitudes, and motivations. You don't say manipulative things unless you are a manipulative person. Don't you want love, and trust, and honesty in your relationship? Do you really think your partner will trust you if you are prone to manipulating him? Manipulation requires deceit and deceit is

Tame Your Tongue and Transform Your Relationship

opposite to honesty. The good impression you made early in the relationship cannot last if your heart is deceptive. The insensitivity of your careless tongue reveals that you have little, if any regard, for his feelings. Why should he take care of you and your feelings if it is not in your heart to do the same thing for him? What is in your heart will come out in your speech and behavior.

"The good man brings good things out of the good stored up in his heart, and the evil man brings evil things out of the evil stored up in his heart. For out of the overflow of his heart his mouth speaks." (Luke 6:45) [NIV]

Another reason to tame the tongue is that your words are indicators of your spiritual maturity. Your words reveal if you focus on yourself or if you focus on God and others. At times our words are right and pleasing to God, but at other times they are violent and destructive. Which of these communication styles reflects our true identity? Someone who is wise and spiritually mature speaks graciously. Her words bring honor to herself and to God. Foolish words, on the other hand, destroy the one who speaks them for the trap she sets for someone else backfires and she becomes trapped instead.

"What the wise say brings them honor, but fools are destroyed by their own words." (Ecclesiastes 10:12) [Good News Version]

The tongue gives us a picture of our basic human nature. When focused on self, we often use words that are cursing to others. However, when focused on God, our words are words of thanksgiving and praise to God and words of encouragement and kindness to others. Before you speak, ask, is what I want to say true? Is it necessary? Is it kind?

> "Avoid godless chatter, because those who indulge in it will become more and more ungodly." (2Timothy 2:16) [NIV]

No matter how spiritual we may think we are, we all could benefit from increased control of our tongues. In today's world, it is deemed acceptable by some to tear people down verbally or to get back at them when we feel they have wronged us. In God's kingdom, insults and revenge are unacceptable. Rise above revenge and pray for those who hurt you instead. God works to change us from the inside out. When the Holy Spirit purifies a heart, He gives self control so that the person will speak words that please God.

> "With the tongue we praise our Lord and Father, and with it we curse men, who have been made in Gods likeness. Out of the same mouth come praise and cursing. My brothers, this should not be." (James 3:9-10) [NIV]

Finally, it is important to tame your tongue because a tamed tongue helps you establish and maintain a healthy relationship. On my CD "Healthy Relationships:

Tame Your Tongue and Transform Your Relationship

Plain and Simple"*, I discuss seven factors that are essential to a healthy relationship. They are:

1. wholeness
2. compatibility
3. open and honest communication
4. trust
5. commitment
6. responsibility
7. chemistry

No one should enter into a relationship unless they are whole. That means, all wounds should be healed and emotional bags unpacked. Healing takes place from the inside out. When God cleans your heart, clean speech is sure to follow. It is easier to speak with a caring tongue when you are compatible with the person. Your interest in the person should help you to, at least, be controlled in your speech. Having things in common will lead you to be pleasant and trustworthy when you speak. Open and honest communication needs to be tempered with compassion. If you are being conniving or careless you are not being open, honest, or compassionate. Your communication is faulty, at best.

Without achieving the first three factors, factor number four, trust is just a pipe dream. When trust exists in a relationship, you share your feelings, emotions, and reactions and have the confidence in your partner to respect you and not take advantage of you. This sharing takes place with the belief that the other person will not share what you have expressed indiscriminately. Trust enables you to place confidence in another so he or she will be supportive and reinforcing of you, even if you let down your mask of strength and show your vulnerabilities.

There can be no trust in a relationship when one or both individuals are not whole. If you do not have similar values, goals, and interests you may always question the motives of one another. And, needless to say, if you are not communicating or if your communication is deceptive, there can be no trust.

Being committed means doing what you say you will do. Can one who is hypocritical, deceitful or malicious do this successfully? Can one who is reckless, self-centered, and insensitive to others be committed? Taking responsibility for our feelings helps us to eliminate the need to blame and retaliate. And of course, passion when coupled with care and love, leads us to want to know what to say and how and when to say it.

If you cannot have the seven factors without a tame tongue and you cannot have a healthy relationship without the seven factors, then it stands to reason that you cannot have a healthy relationship without a tame tongue. Why tame your tongue? Because the tongue has the power of life and death.

*For information on how to purchase see Appendix 2

Chapter 8
How to Tame Your Tongue

"But no man can tame the tongue."
James 3:8a, NIV

How can we expect to tame our tongues when God's Word says it is impossible for any man to do this? If no human being can control the tongue, should we even bother to try? Even if we may not achieve perfect control of our tongues, we can still learn enough control to reduce the damage our words can do. Remember that we are not fighting the tongue in our own strength. The Holy Spirit will give us increasing power to monitor and control what we say, so that when we are offended, the Spirit will remind us of God's love, and we won't react in a hateful manner.

We spend too much time seeking the love of a man. A man who finds a wife finds a good thing. Our time would be better spent seeking God's love. A man will hurt you. This is not male-bashing; it is fact. We are all humans and we hurt one another. God's love, however, never hurts. When you are criticized, what better time to reach out to God? His Spirit will heal the hurt, and you won't lash out in retaliation to the one who hurt you. You have an option: "Rewrite the story" of what took place and take hurt completely out of the script. Respond in love.

In every situation, there are at least three factors that contribute to your response. There is the event or the thing that happened. There is your interpretation of the event. This is a story that you make up in your head. It is based on your education, past experiences, how you were raised, what you value, and a lot of other things. That is why two people can participate in the same event and have different interpretations about what took place. Once they run the event past their own personal experiences and values, they come up with their own unique story about the event. This is an intellectual interpretation. The third factor that contributes to your response is your emotional interpretation which results in feelings.

Here are some examples of how that works. I met a man named David. That was an event. I evaluated David against my image of the ideal man based on my education, past experiences, and values. The "ideal man" is a story that I made up. Who can really say what is "ideal"? We are all made in the image and likeness of God. God's image is not a physical one, but it is the only image that is ideal. The story I wrote about David is that he was overweight and unattractive. I justified the thought that he was overweight with my educa-

Tame Your Tongue and Transform Your Relationship

tion, past experiences and values. I knew enough to know that, for health reasons, there is an "ideal" weight range based on age and height. So, in my mind, I was not being judgmental because there was data to support me. I further justified my thought with past experiences. I knew that I had always been more attracted to men with a certain physique. I knew the importance of being physically attracted to any man that I dated, so I used compatibility and chemistry as an excuse.

Lastly, we all have values. I valued a certain body type. What's wrong with knowing what you like? Without realizing it, I wrote an entire story about David's weight.

Although it is painful to admit, I had an image of who I was and the type of man I "deserved" to be with. This was a pride issue; my pride issue. If David didn't look and dress the part that fit "my image," what would people think of me and my ability to get a good catch? Wow! Did I have that wrong or what? Oh, don't go there. You know you've had a similar reaction to some kind, sweet brother who wanted to get with you, but did not look the part! I let my story cause me to respond to David with a conniving tongue.

Lance told Cheryl there were only two tickets for the show. He made a statement. That was the event. Cheryl wrote a story about that event. In her story, Lance let her down (her interpretation), he chose to bring in the new year with Vicky (his fiancé, duh!) in-

Dr. Linda G. Wiley

stead of bringing it in with Cheryl; he didn't care about Cheryl. All of that was Cheryl's made up story. She didn't know if any of that was true. She didn't know how hard Vicky and Lance may have tried to get tickets or how bad they may have been feeling. And, the truth is, she probably didn't care. Cheryl's emotional interpretation led her to be angry and feel rejected. She chose to feel that way when she wrote her story. Then she chose to respond with a careless tongue.

It would serve you well to separate events from the stories that you write about them and the feelings you attach to your story. Practicing that will take you a long way to taming your tongue. Pray for and practice a calm attitude. Disturbing situations will remain disturbing as long as you are disturbed. But when you become peaceful, conditions will begin to iron themselves out.

If you desire to eliminate careless and conniving speech, the following steps will help.

Step 1: If you are not sure if you speak with a careless or conniving tongue, then you first need to ask the people in your life if they find that the descriptions fit you.

Step 2: Once you are clear that your tongue is careless or conniving whether by the assessment you took in Chapter 2 of this book, by direct feedback from the people in your life or by their reactions, then you need to identify the things you say that make your tongue careless or conniving. Make a list of the offending words, expressions, and tones. It would also be helpful to make a list of the surrounding circumstances (e.g. time of day, location, feelings).

Step 3: After you have identified your offending characteristics, then determine if you are intentionally or unintentionally behaving that way. It is important to be realistic with yourself and acknowledge you can be offensive to others even if you don't intend to be.

Step 4: Assess the negative impact and negative consequences of your intentional or non-intentional behavior on the people you identified in step 1 above.

Step 5: After assessing the impact of your tongue, you next need to assess what if any irrational, unhealthy, and non-reality-based thoughts and beliefs contribute to your behavior. For example, what messages did you receive growing up (e.g. put downs, insults)? How were you rewarded? How were you punished?

Step 6: Now identify healthy, rational, and reality-based thoughts which will contribute to the cessation of your need to be careless or conniving with your tongue

Step 7: Identify new words, expressions, and tones you can use to reduce the negative impacts they experience as a result of your present tongue.

Dr. Linda G. Wiley

Step 8: Identify what you could do to lessen the non-intentional negative impact your tongue has on others. Consider things such as pausing before you speak, speaking encouraging words, practicing gentleness and kindness. For more ideas, read the characteristics of the controlled and caring tongues and emulate what they do.

Step 9: Now you are ready to inform each person who has experienced your negative tongue that you want the behavior and its impact to stop. You can ask for their help. Ask them to give you feedback and "call you on it" when you get off track.

Step 10: Begin to initiate the new behaviors and strategies which you identified above.

Step 11: Monitor the response you are receiving from the people in your life and continuously solicit feedback from them.

Step 12: If people in your life still find you careless and conniving with your tongue, then return to Step One and begin again.

How can you expect to tame your tongue? Jesus gives you the answer: "But with God all things are possible" (Matthew 19:26b) [NIV]. You can no more tame your tongue by yourself than a wild horse can tame itself. Wild horses are tamed by experienced trainers who break them. And the Holy Spirit is our trainer. Only He can break our unruly, wild tongues!

Tame Your Tongue and Transform Your Relationship

This process is most effective when it takes place in the proper context. If you are going to be effective at taming your tongue, it is not enough to implement the steps. There are other conditions that are required.

1. **A personal relationship with Christ:** This is the acceptance of Jesus Christ as your personal Lord and Savior. Acknowledge His greater strength, wisdom, and knowledge and let it guide you through whatever you will encounter in life. Rather than believing that you are 100% in control of your destiny, believe in God's power. This lets you accept God's will in your life and enables you to "let go and let God."
2. **A healing environment:** This is creating and maintaining a healthy relationship with the significant others in your personal life where the characteristics of careless and conniving tongues do not exist.
3. **Reducing a sense of competition:** Reducing competition, jealousy, and defensiveness with significant others in your life is a way to reduce the barriers between you and them. Lowering these psychological barriers is essential for movement toward the development of mutual trust.
4. **Self-acceptance:** Accepting who you are and your potential is an important step in letting down your guard enough to develop a trusting relationship with others. If you are so insecure in your identity that you are unable to accept yourself

first, how can you achieve the self-revelation necessary to develop trust?
5. **Self-disclosure of negative self-scripts:** Disclosing your inability to feel good about yourself and your perceived lack of healthy self-esteem are essential in reducing miscommunication or misunderstanding between you and the significant others in your life. This self-disclosure reveals to the others your perspective on obstacles you believe you bring to relationships. This sheds the mask of self-defensiveness and allows the other to know you as you know yourself. It is easier to trust things that are real versus those that are hidden or unreal.

Through it all, pray for guidance, especially before difficult or emotional conversations, and believe that direction is being given to you. You must believe that this guidance from God can be trusted. Depend on it because God will not fail you.

Tame Your Tongue and Transform Your Relationship

Reflections

1) The tongue that best describes me is the _____ tongue.

2) Some characteristics of this style include

_____

_____

_____

3) My style impacts others by

_____

_____

_____

4) To become more positive in my communications, I commit to

_____

_____

_____

Afterthought

Tame Your Tongue and Transform Your Relationship

A 92-year-old, well-poised and proud man, who is fully dressed each morning by eight o'clock, with his hair fashionably coifed and face shaved perfectly, even though he is legally blind, moved to a nursing home today. His wife of 70 years recently passed away, making the move necessary. After many hours of waiting patiently in the lobby of the nursing home, he smiled sweetly when told his room was ready.

As he maneuvered his walker to the elevator, I provided a visual description of his tiny room, including the eyelet sheets that had been hung on his window. "I love it," he stated with the enthusiasm of an eight-year-old having just been presented with a new puppy. "Mr. Jones, you haven't seen the room; just wait." "That doesn't have anything to do with it," he replied.

"Happiness is something you decide on ahead of time. Whether I like my room or not doesn't depend on how the furniture is arranged; it's how I arrange my mind. I already decided to love it. "It's a decision I make every morning when I wake up. I have a choice; I can spend the day in bed recounting the difficulty I have with the parts of my body that no longer work, or get out of bed and be thankful for the ones that do.

"Each day is a gift, and as long as my eyes open I'll focus on the new day and all the happy memories I've stored away. Just for this time in my life. Old age is like a bank account. You withdraw from what you've put in.

"So, my advice to you would be to deposit a lot of happiness in the bank account of memories! Thank you for your part in filling my memory bank. I am still depositing." Remember these five simple rules to be happy: 1. Free your heart from hatred. 2. Free your mind from worries. 3. Live simply. 4. Give more. 5. Expect less.

About the Author

Dr. Linda G. Wiley is a well-rounded professional dedicated to transforming people's lives. A renowned relationship specialist, author and life coach, Dr. Wiley combines her personal experiences with her passion for relationship counseling to help women in transition transform their lives through healthy relationships within themselves and with their mates.

Noted for her uncanny ability to tap into the very root of relationship issues, Dr. Wiley (under the name of Dr. Owens) has created a CD, "Healthy Relationships: Plain & Simple" with The Motivator Les Brown and "What Every Single Woman Should Know: Dating" with motivational speaker Ona Brown. Additionally, she is a co-author of *Giving Gratitude*, part of the best selling series *Wake Up…Live the Life You Love*. She has now penned a work of her own, *Tame Your Tongue & Transform Your Relationship*.

In addition to her role as an author, Dr. Wiley is a motivational speaker in the Les Brown Speaker's Network and was formerly co-host of Atlanta's V-103 "Love and Relationships" program. She has also appeared on Atlanta television programs In Contact, A Woman's

Dr. Linda G. Wiley

Place and Peachtree Morning as well as the Herbert Dennard Show in Macon, GA. Her perspective has also been heard on New York's WBLS-FM and WRKS-FM, WAMJ-FM and WPZE-FM in Atlanta, WMJJ-FM in the nation's capital, and V-103 of Chicago.

Dr. Wiley is an entrepreneur. As founder and president of The Owens Group, Inc., an innovative performance improvement company that specializes in leadership development and diversity management, she has worked in the U.S. and abroad developing and delivering interventions for clients of all sizes and disciplines from individuals to Fortune 500 companies.

A graduate of Smith College in Northampton, Massachusetts, Dr. Wiley holds a B.A. in Psychology with a minor in Education. She earned an M.A. in Psychology at the University of Hartford in West Hartford, Connecticut and an M.A. and Ph.D. in Organizational Behavior and Organizational Psychology, respectively, from the California School of Professional Psychology in Alameda, California.

She is a member of several professional organizations.

Tame Your Tongue & Transform Your Relationship: The Workshop

I'm sure as you were reading, you thought of several people who need a copy of this book. Well, don't just sit there. Order them a copy! And don't stop there.

Contact Dr. Wiley and have her conduct a Tame Your Tongue & Transform Your Relationship Workshop at your church, your school, your civic organization, your job, your family reunion, or anyplace else.

As a speaker in the Les Brown Speaker's Network, Dr. Linda Wiley knows how to deliver an impactful message sure to get the job done. For more information on how to have a customized workshop for your group contact Dr. Wiley at

HYPERLINK "mailto:Linda@drlindawiley.com"
Linda@drlindawiley.com
Or
mail in the order form below

Name _____

Address _____

_____

Phone (_____) _____

e-mail _____

    I am interested in more information on hosting / attending a Tame Your Tongue & Transform Your Relationship Workshop.

Tame Your Tongue and Transform Your Relationship

In this complex world of relationships,
Dr. Linda (Owens) Wiley gives you tips to make your relationships plain and simple.

With the help of motivational speaker, Les Brown, Dr. (Owens) Wiley tells you the 7 factors necessary for a healthy relationship.

This CD will truly help you.

What if you could listen in on a private conversation between two women who have earned a reputation for influencing people's lives by changing their relationships?

Well, you can!
Dr. Linda (Owens) Wiley and Ona Brown (daughter of motivational speaker, Les Brown) share their perspectives on what every single woman should know about dating. This is one conversation that you ladies – and gentlemen – don't want to miss!

Order this CD today.

Order online at HYPERLINK "http://www.drlindawiley.com" www.drlindawiley.com

Order your copy today!

Dr. Linda G. Wiley

From the best-selling Wake Up . . . Live the Life You Love Series comes the book "Giving Gratitude".

In these pages, you will read of the many reasons Dr. (Owens) Wiley and the other authors such as Dr. Deepak Chopra and Dr. Wayne Dyer have to express gratitude. You will learn how expressing gratitude will create more reasons for you to be thankful.

WE HAVE SPECIAL RATES
FOR BULK ORDERS!

Need a valuable resource for an upcoming seminar?
Looking for a gift for ministry leaders or Sunday School teachers?
A great Thanksgiving gift or Christmas stocking stuffer!

Tame Your Tongue & Transform Your Relationship

© 2011, Linda G. Wiley, Ph.D.   PAGE 72
DATE \@ "M/d/yyyy" 5/24/2011

"...but be ye transformed by the renewing of your mind."
Romans 2:2b (NIV)

Made in the USA
San Bernardino, CA
12 August 2015